Why Won't God Talk to Me?

Surprising Ways He Already Is

By Jenni DeWitt

Why Won't God Talk to Me?

Surprising Ways He Already Is

Copyright © 2014 by Jenni DeWitt

All rights reserved. This book, or any part of this book, may not be reproduced or transmitted in any form or by any means, electronic or mechanical, including photocopying, recording, or by any information storage and retrieval systems, without the written permission of the publisher, except where permitted by law. Reviewers may quote brief passages in reviews.

THE HOLY BIBLE, NEW INTERNATIONAL VERSION®, NIV® Copyright © 1973, 1978, 1984, 2011 by Biblica, Inc.™ Used by permission. All rights reserved worldwide.

Editor's Note:

All people and spiritual relationships are unique and this book is not intended to instruct on means to achieve a desired relationship with God. The guidance offered herein has worked for the author, and our hope is that it can be of use in building your own relationship with God. However, we cannot guarantee this is your path to God.

For Justin, Anthony, and Cooper

Read more by author Jenni DeWitt at:
www.genuflected.com

Contents

PREFACE

INTRODUCTION

GOD IS TALKING

OBSTACLES TO HEARING GOD

   Guilt Over the Past

   Repeat Offender

   Feelings of Unworthiness

HEARING GOD'S VOICE

   1. Hearing God by Doing

   2. Hearing God Through Christian Meditation

   3. Hearing God Through Contemplation

   4. God Speaks to Us Through Others:

   5. God Speaks to Us Through the Witness of Children

   6. Discerning Messages from God

   7. Hearing God Through Music and Worship

TAKE TIME TO NOTICE

   Daily Reflection

   Pay Attention

CONCLUSION

PREFACE

Do you ever feel like the Big Guy is giving you the silent treatment? You keep pouring your heart out, but He's giving you the cold shoulder. All you want is a little guidance, or at least SOME sign that He is actually up there.

Apparently He's talking to other people. You hear them say things like, "I just feel like God is telling me [enter amazing guidance or comfort]."

So what's the deal? Why won't God talk to you?

Well, I think God already IS talking to you. The trick is knowing how to listen. In this book, through practical, down-to-earth explanations and real-life examples, you will learn how to start hearing God. Once you know how to listen, I think you will be amazed at what you hear.

INTRODUCTION

Like many people, I always thought it would be kind of neat to hear the voice of God. However, I never gave the concept too much thought or attention. After all, I was pretty busy living my life.

I was happily married to my husband, Justin, and after years of trouble with infertility, we finally had two healthy boys: Tony who was five and Cooper who was two.

I had stayed home with the kids when they were younger, but as they got older I went back to the working world where I was excelling at my new career in Health Information Management at the local hospital in our small Nebraska town. Life was good.

Every day the kids went to daycare, and my husband and I went to work. We raised our family, paid our bills, and filled our dreams with what big purchase we could make next. There didn't seem to be a lot of motivation to hear God's voice.

Then my 2-year-old son was diagnosed with leukemia. Suddenly we found ourselves just trying to survive this life - literally and physically.

In our struggles, I found that communication with God became a necessity. And instead of treating it like a fun hobby, I moved it up on my list of priorities. I paid attention.

And the more I did, the more I was amazed at how God was there in the midst of everything. He was communicating with me in ways that I had never realized, and not only that, He had been there the WHOLE time.

Through the years and much heartache, my ears were opened. By the grace of God, I started to understand that God had been talking to me in different ways throughout my life. And through observation, I started to realize that God talks to us ALL in different ways at different times in our lives.

Being able to hear God's voice is what helped me survive the most traumatic experience of my life - my son's battle with childhood leukemia. Now I want to share with you what I have learned in the trenches of that suffering.

I want your ears to be opened to the wonderful gift of hearing God's voice. It can change your life and re-ignite your faith in ways you've never dreamed.

GOD IS TALKING

When you think of God talking, what comes to mind? Moses and the burning bush? A big booming voice from heaven? A whisper in the silence?

These are all ways that we have read about in the Bible. Extraordinary stories of God communicating with those He created. But it's not the ONLY way that God communicates with us.

As you've probably noticed, God created all of us very differently. From the way we look to the way we act, not one person is exactly like another. Likewise, the way we speak to God in prayer is as unique as we are.

So why would we think that God talks to us all in the exact same way?

Even *we* change our methods of communication depending on who we are talking to - whether it is a child, a new friend, spouse, or parent. We make subtle adjustments, often without even thinking about it.

It is logical then that God, in all His wisdom, makes perfect adjustments when He communicates with us.

God innately knows us. He created us, and He knows how we are most likely to be able to hear Him. But in our simplicity, it may still take us years to figure out how to hear God, even if He is coming to us in the perfect way.

Okay so God talks to us differently, but that doesn't mean He talks to *everyone*, right? Wrong.

God loves each and every one of us beyond our understanding. We read it over and over in the Bible.

He compares Himself to a shepherd who will leave His entire flock to go in search of one lost sheep. Or a woman who stays up late sweeping the entire house until she finds the lost coin. God makes it clear that He loves us *all* beyond measure.

In fact, the entire New Testament centers around the love story of God sending His only Son, Jesus, to save us. And Jesus didn't come only to save the elite, He came for everyone.

Jesus made that pretty clear when He hung out with fishermen and tax collectors rather than just kings and leaders of the church.

So why do we think that God will only talk to a few chosen, elite people?

Maybe it's because often there are obstacles that stand in our way when we try to hear God's voice. Once we shed some light on these obstacles, it will be easier to work around them.

OBSTACLES TO HEARING GOD

When we feel absence or distance from God, often times we blame God for the gap. We feel like, for one reason or another, He has abandoned us. But in all actuality, God does not move. He is a constant, and He is always there.

The problem originates on our end. We start to pull away or put up walls.

So let's talk about a few obstacles that may come between God and us. If you find that you can identify with one or more of them, try not to worry. As the saying goes, "Admitting you have a problem is half the battle." So just by recognizing the obstacles you are on your way to overcoming them.

GUILT OVER THE PAST

We are all born as beautiful, innocent, little children. But who among us has not been somehow corrupted by this sinful world and our own bad choices?

God sees our pain and our sin, and He tells us over and over that our sin isn't enough to hold us away from Him. The God who came to us in Jesus would never allow something as trivial as sin to come between Him and us, His beloved. If you ask for forgiveness, you are forgiven.

I believe God says, "Please don't allow the sin that you hold against yourself to stand in the way of a relationship between you and Me. Let Me in to see what the problem is, and I will fix it. I am, after all, the great healer. The one who knows all your hurts. The one with the universal bandage. Let me be with you. Let me heal you. When you embrace those feelings of unworthiness and hold me at arms length, you are refusing the gifts that I am seeking to pour upon you. Child, I love you...let me in."

Apology, or confession of sin, is healing and cleansing. As you would apologize to a loved one whom you have hurt, apologize to God. Then trust that you *are* forgiven, and allow yourself to experience the healing that forgiveness can offer.

God's not an old codger who holds grudges. He is an instant forgiver.

By refusing to move on from your past mistakes, you are actually hurting God, because He longs for a relationship with you. Anything that holds you away from Him hurts Him. So trust that you are forgiven, and forgive yourself.

REPEAT OFFENDER

Sometimes being forgiven isn't enough. Our inability to overcome sin eats at us. We think that maybe we better get our spiritual house cleaned up before we invite God into it. Surely He doesn't want to hang out with us when we are such a mess.

So we post an "unworthy" sign on the door of our hearts, and we don't let Him get too close. We hold God at arms length until that unattainable day when we finally get it all together.

But that day never comes. We are never worthy of God, and He knows that. But amazingly, God loves us anyhow.

God knows *everything* about us and still He loves us with a burning and vast kind of love. God doesn't love us *in spite of* our weaknesses. He loves us, weaknesses and all.

The Bible tells us, "Are not five sparrows sold for two cents? Yet not one of them is forgotten before God. Indeed, the very hairs of your head are all numbered. Do not fear; you are more valuable than many sparrows." (Luke 12:6-7)

To God *you* are His chosen one. You are worthy because HE says you are.

God created you just the way you are. He put you in this world at this point and time, and no matter who you are--atheist, devout Christian, Jew or otherwise--God loves you as much as He loved Moses or any other great prophet.

FEELINGS OF UNWORTHINESS

Sometimes it's hard to believe that the creator of the universe could *actually* give two hoots about us. Who are we really? Just a speck on the cosmic map, a blip on the timeline of eternity.

Many of us spend our whole life wondering if we are really enough. We exert a lot of energy to prove that we are somebody that others might care about.

Let me tell you right now: You are enough.

Do you hear that? You are enough.

Not later, not "if only I..." In God's eyes you are enough *right now*.

Nothing you do can earn or lose God's love. He loves you now and always. There is no need for perfection in order to be loved, when it comes to God. We are His children, and we are loved.

When I think about how we live our lives, I imagine it to be a lot like when my son draws me a picture. With enthusiasm he holds it out saying, "Look mommy, I drew a picture of you!"

My "portrait" is just a circle with a bunch of scribbles. But am I going to chastise him because it is not perfect? No! Out of love for my child, I will accept the scribbled picture. It will be enough just as it is, and I will cherish it.

It is enough, not because it is perfect, but because of my love for my son. In this same way, we are enough not because we are perfect, but because God accepts us with love and cherishes us.

HEARING GOD'S VOICE

So we have worked through some of the common obstacles we may encounter as we seek to hear God's voice. Mainly they involve us holding God at arms length for one reason or another.

Hopefully now that we have shed some light on these obstacles, they will be easier to walk around as we go down this path together in seeking to hear God's voice.

As I stated earlier, I believe God talks to each of us in very different ways. And to take that one step farther, I believe that God talks to us in different ways at different times in our lives.

This makes sense. As we grow and change, the way God communicates with us grows and changes. This does not mean that one way is better than another, just different.

Remember that conversation is a two-way street. While you seek to hear God's voice, please do not forget to hold up your end of the conversation by speaking to God in your own way of prayer. Prayer is the key to building our relationship with God.

If prayer is a new concept for you, please be assured that there is no right or wrong way to pray.

In Romans 8:26-27 we are told, "In the same way, the Spirit helps us in our weakness. We do not know what we ought to pray for, but the Spirit Himself intercedes for us through wordless groans. And He who searches our hearts knows the mind of the Spirit, because the Spirit intercedes for God's people in accordance with the will of God."

So talk to God in a way that feels comfortable. Maybe you want to talk to God as a friend, or maybe you prefer to memorize a prayer that you could say. If you would like a prayer to memorize, Jesus taught His disciples this one:

"This, then, is how you should pray:
Our Father in heaven,
hallowed be your name,
your kingdom come,
your will be done,
on earth as it is in heaven.
Give us today our daily bread.
And forgive us our debts,
as we also have forgiven our debtors.
And lead us not into temptation,
but deliver us from the evil one."
(Matthew 6:9-13)

Prayer could be a book in itself, and there are many great books on prayer such as *Open Mind Open Heart*[1] by Thomas Keating and *The Jesuit Guide to (Almost) Everything*[2] by James Martin.

But this book is focused on hearing God's side of the communication, so let's dig in to the ways that you can hear God's voice.

---

[1] Thomas Keating, *Open Mind, Open Heart* (London: Bloomsbury Publishing, 2006)
[2] James Martin, SJ, *The Jesuit Guide to (Almost) Everything* (New York: HarperOne / HarperCollins Publishers 2012)

1. HEARING GOD BY DOING

Many of us build relationships by *doing* things together. To build a bond, we don't want to sit around and talk. We want to DO something.

In all actuality it doesn't even matter what we are doing together - fishing, working, climbing a mountain, learning a new skill - whatever it is, the important part is sharing an experience. It is not a huge leap to understand that people who enjoy bonding by doing things together would also best grow their relationship with God by doing things with Him. I think God is perfectly comfortable building a relationship amidst our activities.

My husband, Justin, is like this. If I ask him to sit down and have a conversation he will do it. Just like he takes time to sit down and talk to God in prayer.

But the times that our relationship feels the most alive are when we are working together, being active and tackling a task. We love to remodel houses together and work on wood projects.

As we work together, we communicate more naturally than we do at other times.

There are several ways you can bond with God and hear His voice by "doing." I will list a few here to get you thinking:

Invite God into Your Projects

When you are doing a project, make a point to invite God into that project with you. A simple prayer in your own words is all that it takes.

Then remember that you have invited Him, and share the ups and downs of the day-to-day details. It can be a real bonding experience.

Once my husband, Justin, was on a committee that was planning a new building for our Catholic school. The goal was to finish the building before the next school year. Justin was feeling overwhelmed by the time crunch.

In addition to the actual building of the structure, he also had to get the approval of several inspectors as well as the archdioceses. In need of help, my husband turned to God in prayer, inviting Him into the project.

The project went on for months and there were several bumps in the road. Inviting God along on the journey does not guarantee a smooth road, but it does offer a partner –someone to celebrate with when things go well and converse with when problems arise.

When Justin invited God into the project, God turned the experience into a way to build their relationship. They worked through problems together and persevered when things were tough.

In the end, despite the rocky and twisting path, the project was completed right on time, and Justin marveled at how God had brought everything together.

If you are a person who bonds by doing, invite God into your projects, and then enjoy the process with Him.

Volunteer

Another way to connect and feel God communicating with you is by volunteering. Volunteer at a local soup kitchen, join a walk to raise funds for cancer research, or hand the homeless person on the corner a warm hamburger.

That feeling that you get - fulfillment and joy - that is God speaking to your heart. That is God building His relationship with you as you work together. So often when we seek to help others, it is *we* who are given so much.

When speaking of the poor, Mother Teresa was known to say, "Each one of them is Jesus in disguise." She felt God's presence and communication through working with the poor - by caring for God's children.

However, even for Mother Teresa this service did not always come easy. In fact, in an interview she once said, "I don't think that I could do this work for even one week if I didn't have four hours of prayer every day."

Through prayer, she was inviting God alongside her so their relationship could grow by doing together.

We cannot all serve to the extent that Mother Teresa did, but she told us, "If you can't feed a hundred people, then feed just one." Even with that *one*, Jesus will be there among you.

Nature

Another active way that we can hear God is through the enjoyment of nature. I used to be a big fan of the show *Survivor*. I'll never forget the season that seemed to be all about God. There was a big group of people who were always shown holding hands and praying.

Then there was this guy, Ozzy, who was often off by himself climbing trees and swimming in the ocean.

They made him out to be a real villain who never joined in the group prayer. On the grand finale, Ozzy spoke up for himself. He explained to the audience that nature is where *he* finds God.

Looking at that quiet, wild-looking young man, it was no shock that he felt closer to God in nature than he did sitting in a circle holding hands with strangers.

Sometimes we can feel God the best when we are in our comfort zone. For Ozzy, nature was his comfort zone. Nature doesn't require a lot of words. With awe, we can soak up God's love as it seeps into every pore of our body.

Whether it's a breathtaking sunset, the vastness of the ocean, or the serenity of a full moon, in that moment of awe, God is there with us speaking His peace and joy into our hearts.

Creating

God is the ultimate creator. Think about it: He created the world and everything in it.

Can't you just imagine Him creating this world like the great artist He is? A little water over here, a little land over there, throw in some animals and a human and voila!

Then on the seventh day He rested. That's the day I imagine Him standing, hands on hips, with a satisfied look on His face.

We are made in God's image so it shouldn't come as a huge surprise that we also get joy from creating. Inviting God into that creative process can be a great way to grow by doing.

No matter what we are creating - whether it is a child, a beautiful flowerbed, or a remodeled car - when we share in the creative process with God, it can be a way that we hear God's voice.

Then, at the end of a project, we can stand together, hands on hips, with a look of satisfaction as we feel God speaking to our hearts, saying, "Yes, we did that together. We created that together, and it is beautiful and good. I love you. What do you want to create next?"

That feeling of shared joy in creation is God speaking to your heart.

Hear God by doing:

1. *Invite God into Your Projects* - Make a point to ask God to share in your projects with you, and then remember you invited Him

2. *Volunteer* - Serve someone else. That feeling of fulfillment and joy is God there with you

3. *Nature* - Recognize God in those moments of awe at nature

4. *Create* -Invite God to share in the creative process with you, and feel His love as you share in the joy of what you have created together.

2. HEARING GOD THROUGH CHRISTIAN MEDITATION

There is a lot of confusion surrounding the word "Meditation." For many people, when they hear the word, they envision a room full of people sitting around on yoga mats, hands on knees, chanting "Om" with middle and thumb fingers touching.

But this kind of Meditation is very different from the Christian kind. Meditation that is associated with Yoga actually has its roots in the Hindu religion. The belief is that normal consciousness obscures sacred reality. Hence the goal is to suspend rational thought.

Christian Meditation, however, is just the opposite. In Christian Meditation, a person has rational and meaningful communication with God.

According to the *Catechism of the Catholic Church*[3], "Christian Meditation is above all a quest. The mind seeks to understand the why and how of the Christian life, in order to adhere and respond to what the Lord is asking."

It is a time to ponder God's revealed truths as written in the Bible and to reflect on how these truths pertain to our life. As we read the Bible and delve into God's Word, it is important to understand that while the Bible was written by man, it is not man-made.

"Above all, you must understand that no prophecy of Scripture came about by the prophet's own interpretation of things. For prophecy never had

---
[3] *Catechism of the Catholic Church* #2705

its origin in the human will, but prophets, though human, spoke from God as they were carried along by the Holy Spirit." (2 Peter 1:20-21)

The Bible is the inspired Word of God. God instructed men to write down His words for our benefit and guidance. The fact that the Bible is roughly 2,000 years old and still is so relevant emphasizes the fact that it is indeed the Word of God.

On *Relevant.com*[4] Christopher Abel writes, "Your Bible is not just a book. It is your friend. And it is the kind of friend who will be waiting there no matter how much time passes. Your friend is wise. Your friend speaks in whispers through the One who authored it."[2]

With Christian Meditation, you will start to meet this friend that is your Bible.

How to do Christian Meditation

There is no set-in-stone process for Christian Meditation. However, I will describe one possible method to get you started. Over time, you can make adjustments based on what feels natural for you.

Step 1: Choose your Passage

When meditating, you will choose a few verses of scripture - no more than five. The goal is quality of understanding, not quantity of reading, which is why you keep your selection so short.

---

[4] Author: Christopher Abel, Title of Article: What Does the Living Word Really Mean? Date Posted: October 1, 2012
Website: Relevant Magazine

There is no wrong way to choose your scripture. However here are a few ideas:

a. Open the Bible randomly. Then choose your spot either by blindly pointing your finger to a verse or by using the calendar date and current hour to determine your verses.

   So for example if I sit down on the 12th at 2 o'clock and randomly open my Bible to Romans then I would find the 12th chapter 2nd verse of Romans.

b. Choose a book of the Bible that you feel drawn to, and then work your way through that book, meditating on a few verses each time.

c. Download an app. There are several free Holy Bible apps available now that allow you to read your Bible anytime and anywhere. These apps often present a daily verse that is a nice choice for a time of Meditation.

d. Select a favorite daily devotional. You could choose to meditate on the verse used for that days reading. (If you are looking for a great devotional, I recommend *Jesus Calling* by Sarah Young.)

e. Use the gospel reading for the day. Each day of the year has a gospel reading assigned to it. One way to find the gospel for the day is to type "today's gospel reading" into an internet search engine such as Google.

Step 2: Pause for Prayer

The goal is to gain guidance from God while meditating on His word. The best way to do this is to ask Him for help. Ask God for the grace to understand His words in your heart. Your prayer does not need to be formal, just speak freely with God.

Perhaps what you say may sound something like, "God please write these verses on my heart and help me to understand their meaning in relation to my life."

Step 3: Read Your Scripture Slowly

Now it is time to get familiar with your verses. To do this, read your scripture selection very slowly two or three times.

While you read, soak in all the little details that you may have otherwise missed. What thoughts do the words bring to mind - sights, smells, and memories? While you read, pay attention to feelings and emotions that are elicited.

Guided by the words of Scripture, your thoughts may wander. Allow yourself to follow those paths and see what truths may be awaiting you.

Don't be afraid of the quiet as you sit in peace pondering God's word. In the silence He may whisper understanding to your heart.

Step 4: Apply the Selection to Your Life

How is God using these words of scripture to speak His wisdom into your life?

Is there a big decision that you have been trying to make? Is there a conflict that you have been trying to work through or a heartache that you are trying to make peace with?

Allow the scripture to speak directly to what is going on in your life right now. Do you find guidance or healing? Do you feel clarity about the situation?

For example, if I am meditating on this scripture: "Just as the Son of Man did not come to be served, but to serve, and to give his life as a ransom for many." (Matthew 20:28, NIV)

I might apply it to my life in this way: Right now the laundry is piling up, and the housework that I dread is staring me in the face. I wish someone would just come to my rescue and say, "Oh honey, let me do that for you."

But with this scripture I am reminded that we weren't meant to be served but to serve. Jesus served us by suffering for our salvation.

Doing laundry might not be the same as dying on the cross, but to me it is still a form of suffering. I can do this housework to serve others, and then offer up that suffering as a form of prayer.

Suddenly the laundry and housework are ways of serving God, and it makes it all feel more meaningful and less annoying.

Remember that God cares about the details. No matter how small our concerns, He cares. So do not be afraid to bring the everyday, ordinary things to your Meditation. Do not consider anything too "little" to bring to God for help.

You don't need to save up your requests and problems for when you really need help. God's help is infinite; it will never run out!

Be aware that every time you sit down to do Christian Meditation it may feel different. Sometimes you might feel God very clearly speaking to your heart through scripture, and other times you may strain to hear anything. That is okay.

Remember that we hear God in different ways at different times in our life.

Hear God through Christian Meditation:

1. Christian Meditation is hearing God's voice through the Bible

2. How to do Christian Meditation:

Choose Your Passage - pick a few verses of Scripture on which to meditate

Pause for Prayer - ask God to guide your understanding

Read Your Scripture Slowly - focus on the details of your Scripture

Apply the Selection to Your Life - ponder how the scripture applies to your life

3. HEARING GOD THROUGH CONTEMPLATION

The best way for me to explain Contemplation is to ask you to picture your heart as an empty glass. In Contemplation, God pours his love into that glass until it is absolutely overflowing.

According to the *Catechism of the Catholic Church*[5], "Contemplation is a *gaze* of faith, fixed on Jesus. 'I look at him and he looks at me'." [3]

St. Teresa of Avila says, "'Contemplative prayer in my opinion is nothing else than a close sharing between friends; it means taking time frequently to be alone with him who we know loves us.' Contemplative prayer seeks him whom my soul loves." [4]

With Christian Meditation, we use our *mind*. With Contemplation, we use our *heart*. It is an opening up of our soul to spend some one-on-one time with God as we soak in His love for us.

Our role in Contemplation is simply to open our heart to the receiving. Once we are open, then God may choose to come and fill our empty glass with His vast love.

This topic is complicated, so let me give you a more concrete example to clarify this concept of opening our hearts to Contemplation.

Have you ever stayed in a hotel room that had a doorway to an adjoining room? This doorway

---

[5] *Catechism of the Catholic Church, 2715, 2709*

actually has two doors - one on each side. The doors are unique, because there is only a doorknob and lock on one side. The other side is flat.

No one can pass through the doorway unless the doors in both rooms are unlocked by the occupants in each room.

Just because you unlock and open the door on your side, does not mean the people in the adjoining room will open their door. But if they do, then there is the freedom to pass from room to room.

This concept is similar to how contemplation works. We unlock the door on our side, the door to our heart, opening ourselves to Contemplation.

Then we wait. If we are going to enter into Contemplation, God also must choose to open the door on His side.

God's decision whether to open His door has nothing to do with how much He does or does not love us - remember that He loves us all more than we know. Likewise, He also knows the best way that He can communicate with us as individuals.

How to Open the Door of Our Heart to Contemplation:

There are many ways to open our heart to Contemplation. Here are three forms of prayer you can use.

Christian Meditation:

Christian Meditation on the word of God is one way to open your heart to the close union with God that is called Contemplation.

When you feel yourself being filled with gratitude, peace, joy, and love during your time of prayer and Meditation, this may be your invitation from God to settle into those feelings with Him - to sit peacefully in silence and be filled with His love.

Meditation on the Mysteries of the Rosary

The Rosary is a form of prayer designed to help us remember and thank God for the events (mysteries) related to our salvation through Jesus. While the Rosary is traditionally a Catholic practice, people of any denomination can pray the Rosary.

If you want to learn how to pray the Rosary, there are many books, websites, and free apps that can be helpful. Also, your local priest can answer questions and give you more information.

As with Christian Meditation, if you are seeking to open your heart to contemplation while praying the Rosary, you may feel God opening the door on His side as feelings of gratitude, peace, joy, and love start to fill you up.

Centering Prayer:

In Psalm 46:10 we read, "Be still and know that I am God." Centering Prayer is a Christ-centered form of silent prayer that helps us to be still.

With this prayer we choose a sacred word as the symbol of our intention to consent to God's presences and action within us. Then we sit comfortably with our eyes closed and be still with God. When our thoughts wander, we return to the word we have chosen.

If you want to learn more about Centering Prayer visit the Contemplative Outreach website or read Thomas Keating's book, *Open Mind Open Heart*.[8]

Test the Spirits

Some believe that any time you are in a state of Contemplation you are in such close union with God that nothing bad, or evil, could come near you.

While I believe that God can easily protect us, I also believe that the devil is very cunning and would love to trick us and confuse us.

Therefore, any time we feel God is inviting us into this time of Contemplation, it is important to make sure that the invitation is coming from God and not another source.

The Bible teaches us that it is important that we test the spirits: "Beloved, do not believe every spirit, but test the spirits to see whether they are from God, for many false prophets have gone out into the world. By this you know the Spirit of God: every spirit that confesses that Jesus Christ has come in the flesh is from God, and every spirit that does not confess Jesus is not from God. This is the spirit of the antichrist, which you heard was coming and now is in the world already. Little children, you are from God and have overcome them, for he who is in you is greater than he who is in the world." (1 John 4:1-4)

That last line carries a lot of weight - the one who is in us (Christ) is greater than the one in the world (the devil). Jesus has already won the battle. Therefore, all we need to do is proclaim that we are on His team.

One way to do this is to speak out loud three times, even if it is just under your breath, a phrase such as, "Jesus Christ is the Word made Flesh."

After you say this statement, if the invitation to Contemplation continues, you can feel reassured that it is an invitation from God. However, if the feeling flees, and you find yourself a bit shaken, then be glad that you thought to test the spirit. The origin was likely not from God.

Even if you don't totally understand this concept, rest assured that the power contained in Jesus' name will ward off the evil one.

If this concept seems scary to you, I'd like to remind you that Jesus is completely capable of protecting you. Therefore, there is no reason for concern. It is just something we must do to keep ourselves safe. Think of it as putting your seatbelt on when you get in your car.

Hear God through Contemplation:

1. Contemplation is an intimate experience with God in which you feel his love

2. How to Open Your Heart to Contemplation:

Christian Meditation - opening through scripture

The Rosary - opening through pondering the mysteries of Christ

Centering Prayer - opening through silent prayer

4. GOD SPEAKS TO US THROUGH OTHERS

God also speaks to us through the people who He has put in our life. He does this in many ways that might escape our notice if we aren't paying attention. Let's get your brain turning with a list of a few different ways that God may speak to you through others in your life.

Random Acts of Kindness

Have you ever heard a story of complete kindness and love that just lifted your heart and filled you with joy?

For example a few years back there was a story on the news of a police officer giving the shoes off his feet to a homeless person on a bitterly cold night. Or perhaps you read about the strangers who arranged a private plane ride so a little girl battling cancer could get the treatment she needed.

These stories of kindness seem to speak deeply to that part of our heart where God resides, and they bring on those feelings of gratitude, hope, love, and joy.

There may be times in our life when we will be on the receiving end of these random acts of kindness. When our son was diagnosed with leukemia, our family was on the receiving end of one random act of kindness after another.

What a phenomenal way to feel the love of God pouring out through other people and directly into our hearts. In this way, we felt God communicating His love for us, and it built the faith of our entire family.

There are other times in our lives when God moves us to be the ones speaking his words of love by caring for others through loving actions.

You'll know what I mean if you have ever had an idea pop into your head such as, "Oh I should pay for that person's meal." or "I should write a note to my great aunt who is in the hospital."

When you get that little tug on your heart to do something nice for someone, DO IT! That may be God asking you, "Will you do this for Me? My children are hurting. I want to use you to bless them with kindness."

If I had to guess, I'd say that you have followed through on some of God's promptings without even realizing it. Take a moment to think of the last time you did some random act of kindness. Did you feel joy, hope, gratitude, peace? Whatever you felt, it was good, right?

I think that is God's way of saying, "Thank you for helping Me take care of My children."

Whether we are on the giving or receiving end, participation in a story of kindness can help us to feel God's presence and love.

Amazing "Coincidences"

There are times when God is using us for His good, and we don't even realize it. I had this experience recently with a friend.

We were talking on the phone while she drove to her father's house. As she arrived, we hung up, and I busied myself with putting away dishes.

When I glanced out the window I saw the most amazing phenomenon. It was one of those clouds that look like a channel straight from Earth to Heaven. But I had never seen one that looked quite like this.

The sun was setting and this channel was illuminated bright orange. As I looked on in awe, a thought popped into my mind, "Wow! God must be taking somebody pretty special to heaven."

As soon as I had the thought I wondered, "Where did that come from?" But the channel was so beautiful that I went and retrieved my camera to take pictures. Little did I know, at that very moment my friend was finding her father dead on the floor of his home.

Later I sent my friend the picture and told her the story. She was comforted. She felt it was God's way of assuring her that her alcoholic father was no longer suffering with addiction but was home with his Father in Heaven.

I was so grateful that God had allowed me to play a role in bringing His message of comfort to my friend. The experience built my faith and opened my eyes to how God can speak to us through the amazing coincidences He orchestrates in our lives.

Just What you Needed to Hear

Have you ever been in a lot of emotional pain, and a friend said something that touched your heart almost on a spiritual level?

Or maybe you were struggling with an important decision and a friend gave you the perfect advice. In times like these, the Holy Spirit could be speaking to you though your friend.

In the Bible, several times we learn that the Holy Spirit inspires God's people to speak His words.

For example, when Jesus asked his disciples who people said He was, we read, "Simon Peter answered, 'You are the Messiah, the Son of the living God.' Jesus replied, 'Blessed are you, Simon son of Jonah, for this was not revealed to you by flesh and blood, but by my Father in heaven.'" (Matthew 15:16-17, NIV)

The Holy Spirit moved Peter to speak these words.

Another time Jesus tells his disciples: "When they bring you before the synagogues and the rulers and the authorities, do not worry about how or what you are to speak in your defense, or what you are to say; for the Holy Spirit will teach you in that very hour what you ought to say." (Luke 12:11-12, NIV)

In these verses we learn that the Holy Spirit can inspire us to speak God's words. When our friends say something that seems to come from the lips of God Himself, then that could be God's way of speaking His love into our hearts.

Media Brings the Message

Have you ever been browsing at the bookstore when suddenly a book seems to leap off the shelf at you?

The summary sounds interesting so you buy it. When you get home and start reading, you are amazed. It's exactly what you needed to hear, and it gives you clarity and peace.

Or maybe you felt compelled to buy a book years ago, and then it sat on your shelf until one day you were drawn to it. Again, when you start reading, you can't believe how perfectly it speaks to your life. It was just what you needed to read at the moment.

God is using the media other people created to communicate His message to you. He knows how you learn best, and perhaps this is the perfect way to speak to you.

In a similar way I believe God can use well-timed movies, blog posts, magazine articles, or even TV shows to send His messages to us. These sources of media can speak to us and give us clarity on our life when they are orchestrated by God.

Hear God Through Others By:

1. *Random Acts of Kindness* - giving or receiving acts of kindness
2. *Amazing "Coincidences"* - when God uses our actions to help others
3. *Just What You Needed to Hear* - when a friend says something seemingly inspired by the Holy Spirit
4. *Media Brings the Message* - good timing for the perfect book, movie, or song

5. GOD SPEAKS TO US THROUGH THE WITNESS OF CHILDREN

We learn in the Bible that children are dear to God, and Jesus makes no secret of the fact that we can all learn from children.

"But Jesus called for them, saying, 'Permit the children to come to Me, and do not hinder them, for the kingdom of God belongs to such as these. Truly I say to you, whoever does not receive the kingdom of God like a child will not enter it at all.'" (Luke 18:16-17)

We are to use a child's simple faith as our role model. Children don't seem to have the burden of anxiety, fear, and doubt that tend to stand in the way of hearing God's voice and feeling His guidance. Their hearts are open to Christ and His movements.

I believe that because of their openness and receptivity, sometimes God uses children to speak to us in various ways.

Wise Beyond Their Years

It is no wonder that "out of the mouths of babes" is a popular saying. Kids have a simple truth about them that seems to get to the heart of the matter, finding the truth in the situation. Nowhere is this more evident than when I hear a child discussing faith in their simple wisdom.

Mindy Durias expresses this beautifully on *gravitycenter.com*[6] when she writes about her experiences praying with her children. As she led her kids in prayer and scripture, they would say things like, "I hear God saying I love you, I am with you, don't fear, you are mine, you belong, rest in me, you do not have to try harder."

Mindy said, "My own heart was healing as they affirmed these things which, as it turned out, I really needed to hear."

These moments can happen in the midst of prayer, but also in our everyday life. Not long ago, my friend was having a bad day.

As she sat watching her child play peacefully on the floor, he looked up and said, "Look mom, my tractor is carrying this load just like Jesus carries us." My friend's heart melted as she was reminded that Jesus would help carry her through this day.

For me, personally, God seems to use my kids quite frequently to get messages through my thick skull. Sometimes it is something simple the kids say that helps me understand a complicated question I have been pondering.

Other times, the kids say profound things out of the blue. When that happens, I can't help but think it is the Holy Spirit speaking through them. For example, one day my boys and I were eating breakfast at the dining room table.

---

[6] Author: Mindy Durias, Title of Article: Following my Children to God's Heart, Date Posted: April 22, 2014, Link to Website: http://gravitycenter.com/following-my-children-to-gods-heart/

We all wake up slowly so we were still in our sleepy haze when my 3-year-old randomly blurted out to my 6-year-old, "Whatever you do, give it to God!"

My older son and I looked at him with expressions that said, "Why the heck did you just say that?" My 3-year-old covered his face, embarrassed. It was like he did not know why he said it.

It made enough of an impact that I pondered what he said and eventually went on to write a post — *Give it to God* — on my blog, *Genuflected.com*. That post ended up being a great comfort to many people, all because of something my 3-year-old said.

Parent-Child Relationship

Another way that my children open my heart to hear God is through the parent-child relationship. God is our heavenly parent, and we are His children. Sometimes I have a hard time understanding how God can forgive me when I am so miserable.

But being an earthly parent, I see that even when my kids are naughty I love them more than words could say. This helps me to see how God could love me even though I screw up over and over.

Often, when I am struggling with how God might see a situation, I imagine how I would feel, as the parent, in a similar situation involving my children.

That parental perspective gives me insight into how God might be seeing things. It helps to give me clarity, and it sheds light on the obstacles that sometimes prevent me from hearing God's loving voice.

Children Having Visions and Seeing Angels

You may have heard it said that children can see things that adults cannot. We had an experience in our own family that was really an eye opener to this idea.

At breakfast one morning, my oldest child asked, "Where's dad?" I looked at him as if he might be losing his mind, because at that time of day his father was always at work. I told him, "Honey, your dad's at work, like always."

He said, "Well then who was that guy in bed with Cooper (his younger brother)?"

The hair on the back of my neck stood up. There was no one else in the house but my children and me. With the speed of adrenaline I raced upstairs, but my son was sleeping peacefully, alone, in bed.

Annoyed, I went back downstairs and asked my oldest son what on *Earth* he was talking about.

A little exasperated he said, "Mo-om, there was a guy in bed with Cooper who looked just like dad. He had his legs bent and his arm around Cooper like this." Tony showed me how the person had been laying, with one arm protectively draped over his brother.

There was no explanation for what my oldest son saw, but he was adamant about it. At first it shook me up. I didn't understand it. But now we wonder if he saw Cooper's guardian angel.

Through my son, God communicated a very powerful reminder that there is a spiritual world all around us that we cannot see. I am comforted by the thought that God has sent His angels to protect us.

Some of my friends have had similar experiences with the children in their lives. One such friend had a sister who died of cancer.

A few weeks later, she was unrolling Christmas lights with her 3-year-old granddaughter when suddenly the little girl looked up at the sky and said, "Look Grandma, it's Betty! She's an angel!"

Caught off guard, my friend looked up to where her granddaughter was pointing, but she could see nothing. There wasn't a cloud in the sky, much less a vision of her dead sister.

It would have been easy to brush off this child's excited exclamations as simply an overactive imagination. However, my friend's heart was open, and she took this experience as a gift from God. She felt it was confirmation and reassurance that her sister was safe in Heaven.

On a national level, we are witnessing how one child, Colton Burpo, had a vision that has built the faith of thousands of people. The book and movie about Colton's experience is called *Heaven is for Real*.

Sometimes children, in their innocence, are allowed to see the glories of heaven. These witnesses by our children can bring us great hope and can strengthen our faith.

"Jesus said, 'Let the little children come to me, and do not hinder them, for the kingdom of heaven belongs to such as these.'" (Matthew 19:14)

Hear God Through the Witness of Children By:

1. *Wise Beyond Their Years* - simple but wise statements of children

2. *Parent-Child Relationship* - using our perspective as a parent to understand God's perspective

3. *Children Having Visions and Seeing Angels* - children's hearts are more open; therefore, sometimes they can see or hear things we cannot

6. DISCERNING MESSAGES FROM GOD

Have you ever wondered what God's actual voice might sound like if He decided to speak to you in words?

I think that His voice sounds different to each and every one of us.

If you'd like to know what it might sound like to you, then humor me for a moment. Close your eyes and *think* in your head the sentence, "I am a human."

Now, when you thought that sentence, how did that voice sound?

From my experience, that is the voice that God often uses when He speaks to me. It is the voice of our own thoughts. This is brilliant when you think about it, because any other voice would probably scare us to death.

But it can also be kind of confusing. How are we supposed to know if we are hearing the voice of God or our own thoughts?

That is where discernment comes in. Discernment is the practice of determining if a message is truly from God. There are many ways that a person can seek to discern a message from God. Let's discuss a few helpful ways here.

Has the message been repeated?

As my priest says, "God is persistent." If a message is truly from God, God will repeat Himself multiple times until we understand Him.

The Bible gives us one perfect example in 1 Samuel:

"The boy Samuel ministered before the LORD under Eli. In those days the word of the LORD was rare; there were not many visions.

One night Eli, whose eyes were becoming so weak that he could barely see, was lying down in his usual place. The lamp of God had not yet gone out, and Samuel was lying down in the house of the LORD, where the ark of God was. Then the LORD called Samuel.

Samuel answered, "Here I am." ⁵ *And he ran to Eli and said, "Here I am; you called me."*

But Eli said, "I did not call; go back and lie down." So he went and lay down.

Again the LORD called, "Samuel!" And Samuel got up and went to Eli and said, "Here I am; you called me."

"My son," Eli said, "I did not call; go back and lie down."

Now Samuel did not yet know the LORD: The word of the LORD had not yet been revealed to him.

A third time the LORD called, "Samuel!" And Samuel got up and went to Eli and said, "Here I am; you called me."

> *Then Eli realized that the LORD was calling the boy. So Eli told Samuel, "Go and lie down, and if he calls you, say, 'Speak, LORD, for your servant is listening.'"*
>
> *So Samuel went and lay down in his place.*
>
> *The LORD came and stood there, calling as at the other times, "Samuel! Samuel!"*
>
> *Then Samuel said, "Speak, for your servant is listening."* (1 Samuel 3:1-10)

God did not share His message once, then roll His eyes, and move on when Samuel didn't get it. God was persistent. Furthermore, God spoke in a voice that was familiar and comforting to Samuel--his mentor, Eli.

God created us, and He knows our limitations. If God has a message for us, He will persist until He conveys that message.

Think back over your life. Can you remember a time when something kept coming back to you until you finally listened?

Just recently I had an experience that shaped my life. I was in the church, praying, "God I have so much anxiety. I just want to hand this all over to you and finally learn to trust!"

As I was praying, I kept hearing, "You are enough." Over and over it repeated. At first I was a little frustrated, because I felt like it was off topic. It was the voice of my thoughts, but it didn't feel like I was thinking it. Instead it felt like someone was saying it to me.

Finally I said, "Okay, thanks, but we are talking about my anxiety here. Remember? And my trust issues, don't forget about those."

But the message persisted: "You are enough."

After hearing the message several more times, I finally decided to listen. As I turned my attention to this phrase, my eyes were opened. Suddenly I could see that a lot of my anxiety stems from my desire to prove that I am enough.

I want to be a good enough wife and mother. I want my writing to be meaningful enough. I want to make enough money. In striving to be perfect in all these areas, I was running around making myself crazy.

I wanted to please everyone so that hopefully, some day, I could be "enough."

But here God was telling me, "You *are* enough." And finally I got it. To Him, I am already enough. Nothing I can do will make God love me any more or any less. Simply put, I am enough.

My shoulders relaxed and the tension in my forehead eased as I realized what God was telling me. I was grateful that He persisted, even when I was too stubborn to listen at first.

Later I was confiding what happened to a close friend when she gasped and said, "You are kidding me! Just today the priest said those exact same words to me in Confession!"

Here God, as represented by the priest, was repeating Himself once again.

Later that week, as I was scrolling through a social media site, something caught my eye. I stopped to read it and there were those exact words again, "You are enough." Again God was repeating his message so I wouldn't forget.

God is persistent.

Does the message follow scripture and church teaching?

God will never reveal anything to us that is against scripture. So check the message or words of encouragement that you feel you are receiving from God. Are they in line with scripture and teachings?

If you think something in the message may be contradictory, then a red flag should go up. Do a little research. Read your Bible, talk with a trusted person, pastor, or mentor to help get clarity.

In the end, if you decide the message you received opposes scripture or teaching, then there is a chance you misunderstood what God was trying to tell you. Or maybe the message's source was not from God after all.

If you come to this conclusion, try not to beat yourself up. Be grateful that you were conscientious in your discernment. The evil one has made it his business to try to confuse us, and he is good at it.

Perhaps the message wasn't from the evil one but had its origins in your own thoughts. That happens. The important thing is to continue to discern our messages and keep our eyes on Jesus. Then we have nothing to fear.

Is it in harmony with my vocation?

Our vocation is our role in this world. A priest's vocation is to live a celibate, single life. My vocation is to be a wife and mother. God may ask us to do hard things in life; however, He will not ask us to do something that is against our vocation.

So, for example, if you are a single mother of five children and you feel God is asking you to leave your children and become a missionary in Africa, then you would want to really pray about the origin of that message.

Since your vocation is the physical and spiritual care of your children, it is unlikely that God would ask you to do something that would impede your vocation.

Hindsight is 20/20

As the saying goes, hindsight is 20/20. There is just something about looking back on a situation that makes everything seem clearer.

The same is true when we are trying to discern whether a message is from God. When we look back, we have the advantage of knowing the "fruits" of the situation - what became of it? What were the results?

The Bible tells us, "But the fruit of the Spirit is love, joy, peace, forbearance, kindness, goodness, faithfulness, gentleness and self-control. Against such things there is no law." (Galatians 5:22-23)

So did the situation result in these fruits? Did it build your faith or the faith of others?

For example, one day, out of the blue, I had the thought that I should send my friend a very specific book.

It seemed like a good idea, but I figured it'd be one of those nice things I would think about and then never actually do.

Then several days later, the thought popped into my head again. Again, I figured it was a nice idea that would never happen.

A few days later, again, the idea popped into my head. I was sitting at my computer, and with a few clicks I ordered the book and had it mailed to my friend.

I never thought much more about it until the day when I was standing at the funeral of her child. She told me, "We must be on the same wave length, because I had just told my husband I needed to read that book, and then here it came in the mail from you."

When she said that, I listened up. I remembered how the idea seemed to come to me of its own accord. I could clearly see the good fruits in how meaningful it had been to my friend in her time of grief.

With the advantage of hindsight, I was able to discern that it had likely been God prompting me to send that book to my friend.

Deciphering God's voice is a life-long learning curve. While hindsight might not be overly helpful in the moment, it will help us to learn what God's voice might sound like in the future.

The more that we practice, the more adept we will become at discerning the origin of the messages we receive.

Hear God by Discerning Messages:

1. *Has the Message Been Repeated?* - God is persistent in repeating the message
2. *Does the Message Follow Scripture and Church Teaching?* - God will not contradict Himself
3. *Is It In Harmony with My Vocation?* - God won't ask us to do something that interferes with our primary vocation in life
4. *Hindsight is 20/20* - looking back to discerning if the message was from God

7. HEARING GOD THROUGH MUSIC AND WORSHIP

Music and worship, whether experienced together or independently, can be powerful ways to hear God communicating with us.

While these may be more traditional ways of hearing God's voice, their importance cannot be overlooked.

God's Message in the Music

Think about all the meaning and emotion that one song can embody. There are some songs that, upon hearing them, can immediately transport us back to a place and time in our life.

When God chooses to use music to communicate with us, it can be deeply moving. I had a first-hand experience with this, and it changed my life forever.

My husband and I had just been married, and we were trying to decide which church to join. He had grown up Catholic, and I had grown up Lutheran.

We knew we wanted to be united in our religion, but we were pretty much okay with either choice so we were having a hard time making a decision.

One weekend we went to visit my husband's side of the family out of town. I had attended plenty of Masses throughout our dating years (not to mention my previous boyfriend had been Catholic), so I was fairly familiar with how things went.

At one point in the service, we were singing a song that I surely must have sung several times before, but this time tears were streaming down my face.

I could feel this song tug at my heart as God told me, "This way, Jenni. This is where I want you." It was so distinct and real that when I walked out of Mass that day, I knew with absolute certainty that I was going to become Catholic.

My husband must have been shocked when I suddenly told him my decision with such decisiveness. It was difficult to explain the experience to him in words. Oftentimes God speaks to us in ways that are so personal that it is hard to communicate them to others.

Some of the most famous composers of all time, like Bach and Handel, wrote great pieces of classical music for Christian churches. Christian music can be moving, and at first it may seem like the most likely way that God would speak to us through music.

But I don't think God limits Himself like that. I believe that God can speak to us in all genres of music - whether it's a hymn pouring out of organ pipes or a song in the car on our way to work.

One time my friend told me, "I keep hearing this old song on the radio. I hadn't heard it in years, but now I keep hearing it everywhere - in the grocery store, in the car, at work. I don't know why I am hearing it all of a sudden."

I admitted that I hadn't heard the song in years and explained to her my theory that sometimes God speaks to us through music.

Her eyes got big, and then she paused for a moment as she mentally sang back the lyrics in her head. With a gasp of surprise she realized the words to the song spoke directly to a problem she was having in her life.

Through music, God can give us clarity and insight.

Worship

In the Bible, God encourages us to gather together in worship. "For where two or three have gathered together in My name, I am there in their midst." (Matthew 18:20)

God desires us all to gather in worship, although this can take many forms. As you know, with the help of God, I have chosen the Catholic faith. To me, the traditions are so meaningful, and the more I learn about my faith, the more I fall in love with it.

Specifically, I love the reverence given to the Eucharist - the consecrated bread and wine.

It is our belief that when the priest consecrates (or prays over) the bread and wine during Mass, it becomes Jesus' body, blood, soul, and divinity. The only part of the bread that is left is the appearance - *everything* else is Jesus.

Without faith, this is just as impossible to see as a molecule without a microscope, but Jesus is actually there with us. To me that is amazing!

Adoration is another tradition that is very meaningful to me. It is a time where we go into the church and sit with the Eucharist, the consecrated bread that is now Jesus, and we pray. During this time I often feel God communicating with me.

Likewise, Holy Communion--the part of Mass where we receive the Eucharist--is another sacred moment for me in worship where I feel God granting me His peace, healing, and love.

These are examples of how I personally experience God communicating with me through worship. However the experience is so incredibly individual that other Catholics likely hear God through worship in entirely different ways.

You will likely experience your worship service, whatever it may be, in a different way than I do. The diversity of worship styles is just another example of how beautifully God can communicate with each of us in our own way.

Choosing a Church

With all the different ways that God communicates with us, I cannot help but wonder if that is why there are so many KINDS of Christian churches.

It is up to you to figure out which church to attend. But you don't have to do it alone. Pray and ask God for help and guidance in your decision.

If you want to learn more about the Catholic faith, I have found that local priests are happy to answer questions. God knows I have pummeled them with enough of my own over the years!

However, if you would prefer to start your search online, here are a few informative websites to get you started:

http://www.therealpresence.org/eucharst/a.html

http://www.catholicscomehome.org/

http://www.patheos.com/Library/Roman-Catholicism.html

If you are curious about other denominations, the website ReligionFacts.com[7] is rich with information. Among this information is an easy-to-read chart[8] explaining the differences among the Christian faiths.

On catholic-resources.org[9] Felix Just, S.J., PhD has also compiled this nice overview of the main branches of Christianity.

---

[7] www.religionfacts.com/christianity/denominations.htm
[8] www.religionfacts.com/christianity/charts/denominations_beliefs.htm
[9] http://catholic-resources.org/Courses/Christianity-Branches.htm

It may also be helpful to attend church at the different denominations you are considering. This can help discern what's right for you, and give you a feel for which faith intrigues you or makes you feel the most comfortable.

Hear God Through Music and Worship

1. *God's Message in the Music* - sometimes God communicates with us through song
2. *Worship* - when we gather together in God's name, He promises to be in our midst
3. *Choosing a Church* - an individual choice about how we want to worship

TAKE TIME TO NOTICE

Hopefully now you understand a little bit better *how* to listen for God's voice.

But life is hectic. There are deadlines, laundry, lunches, and appointments, and unless we take *time* to listen, we still might not notice how God is communicating with us.

You don't have to wait for a major life crisis to occur before you give communication with God the attention it deserves.

Instead, you can make it a part of your day-to-day life right now. Here are a couple ideas:

DAILY REFLECTION

Daily reflection is a time when we ponder the moments of our day and look for God's hand. How is He working and communicating with us in our life?

Throughout history, people have outlined several formats for this time of reflection. For example, in 1548 St. Ignatius of Loyola popularized the Jesuit way of reflection with his book *Spiritual Exercises*. His method is often referred to as the Examen.

James Martin, S.J. summarizes St. Ignatius' steps for us in his book, *The Jesuit Guide to (Almost) Everything*.[10] Likewise, in his book *33 Days to*

---

[10] James Martin, S.J., *The Jesuit Guide to (Almost) Everything* (New York: HarperOne / HarperCollins Publishers 2012), p. 97.

Morning Glory,[11] Rev. Michael Gaitley gives us another suggestion of how we could examine our daily life using the acronym B-A-K-E-R.

While there are several ways to reflect on our day, here is one to get you started:

Start small:

With physical exercise, doctors recommend that we start small and build our way up. This is a good practice in spiritual exercise as well.

If we try to carve out an hour in our day, it may seem like too big of a drain on our time and energy. As a result we may be more likely to abandon it completely.

So instead, start small with perhaps five or ten minutes a day. As time goes on, you can lengthen your reflection as you see fit.

Choose a time of day that works best:

No matter how much I try to be a morning person, I'm just not. The afternoon and evening is when I am at my best. Over the years, I have learned to quit fighting nature.

I suggest you do the same as you think about when you would like to do your reflection. If you tend to be a morning person, then the mornings might be a good time of day to reflect on the previous 24 hours.

---

[11] Michael E. Gaitley, MIC, *33 Days to Morning Glory* (Stockbridge, MA: Marian Press, 2014), p.188-189

If you are more of a night person, perhaps some time right after work or before bed might be a better option for you. Then again, perhaps you want to split the difference and use your lunch break to reflect on the past 24 hours.

The most important thing is to look at your schedule and find a time that you think would naturally fit best into your current daily life.

Schedule the time:

Once you decide on the time of day, schedule it into your day like any other important event. Then make that time non-negotiable.

We all know things pop up, and so we are sent looking for other events to eliminate. Don't let that happen with your reflection time. This time is vital to your spiritual health, so treat it that way.

Still your thoughts:

The obligations and responsibilities of this world can be oppressive. Consider your time of reflection as your daily vacation. No worries allowed.

This is tough, so ask God for help. Make up your own prayer of request or say this one: "God I'm so grateful to have this time alone with you. Please calm my thoughts and give me your peace. Please guide me as I seek to see your loving hand at work in my life."

There will be times when racing thoughts will burst through the peace. Do not feel bad. Just ask God again for his help and peace, and then trust Him to give it to you. This may take practice.

Express gratitude:

I have found in my own life that gratitude is the quickest way from here to God. We learn from the Bible that God inhabits our praise: "But you are holy, O you that inhabit the praises of Israel." (Psalm 22:3)

So take a few moments at the beginning of your reflection to express your gratitude for the blessings in your life. Then trust that God is there with you - inhabiting your praise.

Reflect:

Now it is time to mentally walk back over the last 24 hours.

Were there any prayers answered? Maybe you received good news or words of encouragement just when you needed them most?

Maybe a project you had been worried about finally came together beautifully? Maybe you experienced the perfection of Holy timing?

God works in many ways. It is up to us to decide if we believe these things are coincidences or "God-incidences" - the hand of God at work in our lives.

Pray:

Conclude your time of reflection with a prayer of your choice speaking to God about what you have noticed in your day. This can be a formal or informal prayer of your choosing.

PAY ATTENTION

It is important to pay attention as we go about our day so that we can spot God in action. But sometimes it is so easy to miss His hand in our day-to-day life.

However, when we keep our eyes open we will start to notice Him more and more. God is present, taking care of our needs, and communicating with us every single day.

This was never more obvious to me than one day when I was driving in the city. I felt like I had spent my entire life sitting at red lights. In an offhand prayer I asked God, "Could you please just give me some green lights here?"

I sped on to my next appointment and really didn't give the prayer a second thought. The next day my husband was driving when he said in an amazed tone, "Do you realize we haven't had one single red light all day?"

I hadn't told my husband about my prayer the day before; I barely remembered it myself. But when he pointed out that we had all green lights, I was reminded.

I laughed out loud with joy at God's answer to my prayer! It was like finding a tiny gold nugget in my day, as I was reminded once again that God cares about the details of our lives.

It is so important to pray about everything, because God cares. If we bring our daily concerns to Him in prayer, we give Him an opportunity to show it.

Sometimes, even when we don't make specific prayer requests, God steps in and gives us special gifts or help. It is good to notice these and give thanks.

While I was writing this book, I had an experience that drove home this point. As I was finishing up the section on Christian Meditation and preparing to move on to Contemplation, the doorbell rang.

It was the delivery person, three hours earlier than normal, bringing me a book that I wanted to reference regarding Contemplation. With gratitude and awe, I smiled with joy realizing the very book I needed had literally just landed on my back step.

I walked back upstairs to get to work, and the moment I sat down, I received a text from a friend. She had come across an article on contemplation that reminded her of me.

It was amazing to me that these two references arrived just when I needed them. Talk about Holy timing!

Seeing God's hand in the smaller matters can remind and reassure us that He is helping us with the bigger problems in our life as well. But the key is to pay attention.

CONCLUSION

For your review, here is a list of the seven ways God may already be talking to you. As you scan through, think about which ways really resonate with you. Then I encourage you to go back and further review those sections.

1. Hearing by Doing - Through experiences, activities, and nature we hear God's voice.

2. Hearing God Through Christian Meditation - By reflecting on scripture we hear God's voice.

3. Hearing God Through Contemplation - In the stillness we hear God's voice.

4. God Speaks to Us Through Others- God uses others to speak His words to us.

5. God Speaks to Us Through the Witness of Children - Through the simple faith of a child we hear God's voice.

6. Discerning Messages - We identify God's voice in our thoughts.

7. Hearing God Through Music and Worship - Through the practices of our faith we hear God's voice.

God is speaking.

Are you listening?

To read more about Jenni's insights on God and life, join her community online at: **www.genuflected.com** or like Genuflected on Facebook.